IMAGES OF ENGLAND

EMSWORTH

IMAGES OF ENGLAND

EMSWORTH

LINDA NEWELL

TEMPUS

for Ernie Newell (1947-2004)

Frontispiece: Ernie was born in Emsworth and lived all his life in the village he loved. He was my love, my support and my meticulous and patient researcher. He did not see the fruition of our joint work. This book is for him.

First published 2006

Tempus Publishing Limited
The Mill, Brimscombe Port,
Stroud, Gloucestershire, GL5 2QG
www.tempus-publishing.com

British Library Cataloguing in Publication Data.
A catalogue record for this book is available from the British Library.

ISBN 0 7524 3823 9

Typesetting and origination by Tempus Publishing Limited.
Printed in Great Britain.

Contents

Acknowledgements

Compiling a book of this nature has proved to be such a joy: the joy of discovery, and, also, of solving puzzles, has kept minds occupied for hours, not to mention voices. All those who have helped me with this quest deserve my profound gratitude. All proceeds from the sale of this book will be going to help preserve the last surviving oyster boat that was built in Foster's yard. She is only one of the harbour vessels and not one of the main ocean-going beauties, but she is still precious to us living in Emsworth. *Terror* will be available to take a few people out into the harbour under sail whenever the wind and weather is suitable. She will be a wonderful evocation of Emsworth's history.

Those I have to thank include my children, Helen and Stephen, for their patience while I worked ideas out on them. I did notice the glazed expressions at times! Their partners – Richard and Claire – have also been very supportive. Especial thanks to you all.

Emsworth people are always happy to talk about their home town and among them were Ron and Rose Barter, Ray and Bonnie Prior, John and Elaine Tweddell, Rosemary Shuker and Anne Dridge, John Voysey, Trevor and Jan Butler, Alice Sugden, Tessa Daines, Sue Silver, Shirley Wenman, Gill Griffin, Viv Williams, Marie Middleton, Shirley Hogben, Jean Gullick, George and Margaret Newell and Rosemary Jupp. If there are any I have missed, I hope they will forgive me and accept my thanks.

My father-in-law Ted Newell, my mother Doreen Bullock and my sister and brother-in-law, Sheila and Brian Privett, have all added their memories and contacts.

Emsworth Museum is a mine of information about the town while Havant Museum provided the context of the town within the area. The staff of Steve, Denise and Jackie are incredibly enthusiastic about local history and long may it continue! Hampshire Museum Service, Library Service and Hampshire County Record Office have also allowed me to use some of the images available on their internet sites: my thanks to Geoff Salter, Wendy Bowen and Linda Champ.

Most of all I have to thank Bernard Gudge for his photographs. His collection is phenomenal and I know that there are still many that we did not get round to studying, as well as adding some to the collection. Hopefully we will have enough material to produce a sequel to this contribution to recording the history of Emsworth.

Echoes of Emsworth

Whenever anyone hears the name of Emsworth they usually think of the sea, of fishing and of oysters. However, that is not the whole of this community. Yes, the sea has played a very important part in the location and development of the town, but if that was all, then Emsworth would be like many of the other villages on the shores of Chichester Harbour. They are beautiful and bustling communities, but are mainly tourist attractions and sailing centres. Emsworth is also beautiful and bustling, but is a living, working and breathing community striding into the twenty-first century with confidence in its own identity and its ability to serve the needs of its resident community.

What made Emsworth different from other communities in the area, and allowed it to prosper, is the fact that there were three distinct sections that developed in the community. Families and individual people crossed between these sections, and some retained links in more than one, but they are very diverse. When one section was not prospering, the others were able to sustain the community.

The obvious part of the town that everyone recognises is the fishing community. Fishing was one of the original reasons that the community developed on this little spit of land between two tidal streams at the top of the harbour. A little farmstead or hamlet with access to the sea grew and developed to the south of the old Roman road that ran from Chichester to Havant, and on to Portchester and Winchester. From the shape of the roads in the middle of the town it seems likely that this original 'worth' or settlement, possibly belonging to Emil, was sited at the top of the slope leading from the shore, well above the tide line and unaffected by storms in the harbour. Where the inhabitants moved around on their little hill, they wore paths and cart tracks in the ground, which joined the Roman road in two places, and also ran down to the water, where they kept their fishing boats. At this time, water travel was far safer and smoother than road travel, so they used the waters of the harbour to keep in touch with other settlements along the harbour's edge. The village of Warblington was the mother community of this little settlement. Gradually the benefits of living in the area between the two streams became obvious, and the villagers from Warblington drifted along the harbour and settled in 'Emil's worth'. No real record of the settlement exists for the period before the early thirteenth century, when William Aguillon was given the village in exchange for the rent of a pair of gilt spurs each year. In 1239 a charter was given to Herbert Fitzherbert, allowing him to hold a market. However, he could not hold the market at Warblington, because the Bishop of Winchester already had a market at Havant, and the Bishop definitely did not want a market so close to his own. Therefore, the market was moved to the little settlement of Emilsworth and this was the real beginning of the community.

Over the centuries the fishermen settled in what is now South Street and along the shores of the harbour. They worked hard and played hard, but their life was a precarious one, and depended upon going out on the boats when the tide was right and the fish were there. They went out in all weathers and caught what they could. Gradually they found that their best commercial catch was the oyster. Until the late Victorian period the oyster was food for the poor, but then the rich, as they will, developed a taste for it, and made it a very fashionable dish. With fashion came a rise in price, and therefore it became the food of the rich and commanded high prices. The Emsworth oyster fishermen had a very seasonal trade, but for quite a long time it was a very lucrative one, with fishermen being able to make a very good living. However, disaster struck: this trade was virtually destroyed with the typhoid scare of 1902. Some of the fishermen were able to work out of other ports, using their Emsworth fishing smacks, and continued to dredge for oysters in the winter and work, during the summer months, on the racing yachts of the rich and famous that were based in Cowes.

However, at no time did they ever make a fortune, and most of their wives would be trying to help with the family finances by doing cleaning work or opening a small general store in the front parlour. Sometimes the front parlour was a beer parlour, but anything to keep the children in clothes and shoes, and to make sure there was something in the larder if the men came home empty-handed – and some of them did not come home at all. Some of the fishing and trading vessels had a crew of five or six men, and it was a cruel event for the whole town when one was lost with all hands. The sea is a fickle master, even in these high-tech days.

Most of these fishing families still have descendants living in Emsworth today. Many people investigating their family history in Emsworth find that they have fishermen in their line, such as the Barter, Prior, Parham, Cole and Savage families. The main fishing families were those who owned their own oyster beds in the harbour or built their own boats. These families tended to cross the boundaries into the other sections of the community, because they became tradesmen and even merchants. The two most successful families were the Fosters and Kennetts.

The second section of the community is the commercial community, made up of the small traders and craftsmen that keep the town fed and looking good. Many of them had started working as fishermen. During the late nineteenth century many of the men were working on the oyster smacks of Mr Foster or Mr Kennett, or had joined the small tramp ships trading between northern Europe, northern Britain and the Solent ports. However, the sea may not have been in their blood and eventually the call of the settled life on land, and marriage (!) led them to open a small shop, dealing in fruit and vegetables, or hardware or groceries or meat, such as Tiers and Treagusts, still in business today, as well as Charles Silk, Thomas Sargant, or James Mant. Successful businessmen could attract enough trade to open more than one shop in the village. George Davis had bakery businesses in Queen Street; one at the top of the hill near the centre of the village, and one at the bottom, close to the little community over the bridge in Hermitage. There were also cobblers, haberdashers, ironmongers, publicans, florists and hairdressers. Alternatively, they may have found a niche in the growing demand for house building and become labourers, or craftsmen, such as the Louch family. There are still examples of their brickwork, plumbing and garden design in Emsworth.

Over the years the roads improved enough to make travel easier by land than by sea, and the road between Chichester and Portsmouth, still following the old Roman road, became an important route. Coaches began to ply their trade between the villages and Emsworth built up a trade in coaching inns, to allow people to stop on the way. The Crown and the Black Dog were popular coach halts, and expanded to provide private function rooms, where parties and balls were held. Many of the clubs and societies had their first meetings in these rooms, before deciding that they needed their own premises.

The third section of the community was those who had made their way in life and were able to live on their savings. They may have been Emsworth people who had worked hard, been lucky or inherited wealth, or they may have been incomers. These people may have retired from the armed forces: there were many retired naval officers living in Emsworth, and there still are. Most of the bigger houses in King Street and Queen Street were built for these people. During the Victorian era the increase in retired people wanting to live in Emsworth meant that houses began to stretch along the roads to the west and north. New Brighton Road was so called because it was thought that this area would rival Brighton in popularity. The King family, who were shipbuilders at the time of Nelson and the Battle of Trafalgar, built their house in King Street, as did the Foster family. The Fosters had many interests in Emsworth for about 100 years from 1850, because James Duncan Foster built some of the best inshore fishing vessels in the country, but he and his brothers were also timber merchants, haulage contractors, sand and gravel merchants as well as oyster and shellfish merchants.

Business can always attract other businesses, and so solicitors and banks opened their offices in Emsworth, and when business flourished they were able to build large premises in the town, and nice houses for their managers. Many of these properties are still in family ownership, and although people retire to Emsworth or start their second career here, they tend to live here as well, so that the community continues to be complete.

The three sections of the community have melded together and formed a cohesive whole. They have always played together at soccer, cricket, darts and bowls; they shared, and still share, their recreation times, whether it is sailing in the harbour or working in their gardens. So successful have these pastimes become that there are two active sailing clubs, which were formed just after the First World War, at either end of the promenade; Emsworth Sailing Club to the west and Emsworth Slipper Sailing Club to the east. The Horticultural Society has organised the allotments for nearly 100 years, and has been the main organiser of the very successful Emsworth Show in August. All the time, new organisations are being formed, and the young people are not forgotten with thriving Scouts, Guides and Girls' Brigade. At the beginning of the twenty-first century we are beginning to think about how we care for our environment. As a consequence conservation areas such as Brook Meadow and Nore Barn have enthusiastic supporters, groups working and planning how to preserve them for future generations. The museum is totally run by enthusiastic volunteers, as is the associated historical society. What is now putting Emsworth on the map again is the Food Festival, three days in September of eating, drinking and enjoying everything that Emsworth has to offer.

This is a community that is bucking all the trends. It is not just a dormitory town for the nearest big city, nor is it a heaving tourist destination where the local people cannot leave their front doors because there are too many people on the pavements and coaches in the car parks. This community in 2005 was sixth in the UK's best non-cloned towns, and has shops of all descriptions, including two butchers, two bakers, two greengrocers and two small supermarket cum general stores. There are florists, antiques, cafés, restaurants, stationers and gift shops as well as three banks, estate agents, building societies and nine pubs. Services include two thriving primary schools, five denominations of church, a bus service, a post office, a fire station and a railway station. All of them are in great working order.

We are very proud of our thriving community and work hard to make sure it maintains its momentum and continues to serve its future residents.

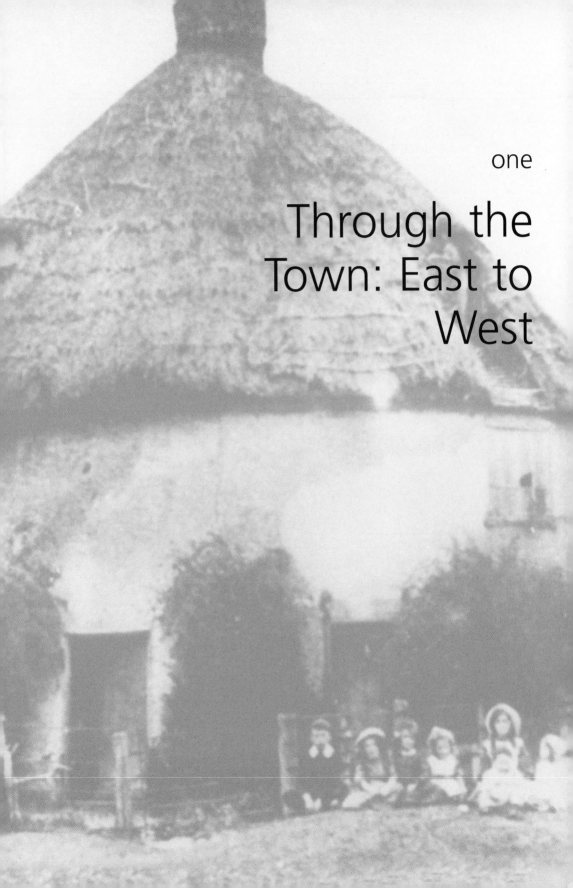

one

Through the Town: East to West

HER MAJESTY.
Passing through EMSWORTH on her late visit to PORTSMOUTH
Feb 28th 1842.

This highly dramatised view depicts Queen Victoria passing through Emsworth in 1842. Her only stop was at the county boundary, where she was welcomed to Hampshire by the Lord Lieutenant of the county, the Duke of Wellington.

Hermitage, to the east, was always considered the poorer part of Emsworth, but it was really part of Westbourne parish. The parish constable of Emsworth had no jurisdiction here, and the Westbourne constable was too far away, so it apparently had a shady reputation. At the top of the hill is the Sussex Brewery, with the rope walk behind, while to the right can be seen the Great Eastern public house, closed in 1917. Just out of the picture, to the left, is the Royal Oak, and beside that was the Lads of the Village, which was demolished in 1891.

This view of Slipper Mill Pond at the turn of the nineteenth century is taken from the rear of the Great Eastern. There is no road along the side of the pond, and the houses on the left have their own sea walls, to protect them from high tides. The chimney to the right is all that remains of the project to build a second mill, with its own mill pond, to the south of the existing Slipper Mill. (Courtesy of Hampshire Record Office – 33M84/16/88)

The Round House was – round! At the southern end of the Hermitage Rope Walk, it was originally a brick-making works. The puddling house was round so horses could be harnessed to work there. When the works closed, the horses had firmed the surface so that no foundations were needed. Therefore it was easy to build a round house, which was, in fact, two semi-circular houses. They were inhabited from the 1840s until 1912, when they were abandoned by the Burgess and Spencer families.

An aerial photograph looking south over Slipper Pond in the 1920s. The River Ems flows into the water to the right, and this was the county boundary for many years. Hendy's Quay, at the end of King Street, can be seen in the middle at the top and was the site of J.D. Foster's shipyard, where he constructed the series of oyster smacks that made Emsworth noteworthy at the end of the nineteenth century. Slipper Pond was an artificial millpond constructed from the outflow from Lumley Mill, which was situated upstream. It served Slipper Mill, which is top left, and drained through a sluice in the wall. Chichester and Hermitage are to the left, with the Royal Oak pub. The Great Eastern pub can be clearly seen. The area to the right of the picture was known as Mud Island, and consisted of houses and small industrial workings. These were all demolished between the wars, and Lillywhites and Border garages were developed. Across the road is the Lord Raglan, yet another Emsworth pub. Beside it is an open space where Chequers garage was built.

Opposite below: A stormy scene looking west from Hermitage into Emsworth. Taken during the 1930s, the photographer is being blown about judging from the blurred focus. All the properties to the right have been demolished. Luckily, there is not much traffic to swamp these cautious cyclists!

Above: Slipper Mill was powered by the tide flowing out of the millpond constructed at the end of the mill stream from Lumley Mill. It was possibly built in the middle of the eighteenth century with an undershot wheel. Milling was possible for about five hours after high tide, so the miller lived by the tide. The mill was built over the water, with storage at right angles on the land. It was in use until the end of the Second World War, when it was used for storage. The storehouse is all that is left and has been converted into housing.

The same area as the previous photograph, but looking east and during the 1960s. Instead of Mud Island there are two garages. The one selling VIP petrol at five shillings halfpenny a gallon is Border Garage, which was next to Lillywhite's. Behind the Mobil tanker was Chequers Garage. The mechanics obviously rescued cars as well as repaired them!

Yet another high tide at the bottom of Queen Street in the 1930s. On the left is the Town Mill, which is reputed to be the site of the original village mill, straddling the River Ems, and powered by water coming down the river. It suffered the fate of many mills, burning down several times, and this building dates from its final reconstruction in 1897. It was later converted to work by electricity.

These beautiful town houses in Queen Street were inhabited by people who had made their wealth as merchants dealing in corn and fish. Daniel Defoe noted that the moneyed men of Emsworth were engaged in the corn trade, which was more important and enduring than fishing. This photograph of 1910 shows that very little has changed over the years.

High St., and Queen St., Emsworth.

Looking in the opposite direction, towards the junction of Queen Street and High Street. Mr Summer's ironmonger shop was in existence until 1899, so this photograph could be one of the earliest ones taken in Emsworth.

Children are always ready to pose for a photograph. All the boys are wearing hats, but not all of them are wearing shoes! This scene is at the junction of Queen Street, King Street and High Street.

Above: A wonderful aerial shot from the 1920s showing the centre of the town very clearly. The pump has gone from the centre of the Square, but the lamp is still there. In the centre bottom the turning from Queen Street can just be seen, and on the left is South Street. The junction of West Street, High Street and North Street is very clear on the top right. The town hall has been converted into a cinema, and the large building in the centre top is the Community Hall, which was the social centre of the town. The entrance was in School Lane, to the right. Running straight from the Square to the top is Nile Street, which was constructed in the early 1820s and named to commemorate the Battle of the Nile, and the original Congregational Chapel has been built on the right hand side of the street: many of the houses along Bridgefoot Path and School Lane have yet to be built. To the right can be seen the jumble of backyards and workshops that had built up behind the shops in High Street, and many of the main buildings show signs that the frontages have been redesigned, but the rest of the building is a lot older. The small triangle of land in High Street, in the centre at the bottom, is reputedly there because there is a well at that point, and building is impossible.

Opposite below: King Street was once known as Sweare Lane, and was the only route to Thorney Island, via the Wadeway. John King developed his shipyard in this area, and was so successful the road name was changed in his honour. His shipyard produced small boats, oars and capstan bars for Nelson's Navy. A press gang tried to impress his workers, but he closed the gates until he had secured exemption for all his men. This view looks down to J.D. Foster's shipyard. (Courtesy of Hampshire Library and Information Service)

Carnival processions were great events: this patriotic display has reached the junction of Queen Street and High Street, with King Street stretching into the distance. The photograph was taken from the upper window of Mr Young's shop.

Emsworth Square, and the shape of the buildings is very recognisable. The large building facing the photographer was demolished in the early 1960s to aid traffic flow from North Street into High Street. The white building to its left was the doctor's house: the orchard was used to build the hospital. It is still the doctors' surgery.

Emsworth Square from the opposite direction. The Crown Hotel on the left is possibly the oldest public house in Emsworth. They had to remove the portico in the 1960s because it was considered unsafe. Mr Bundy's premises, on the right, were a stationery supplier in 1899. It is now Newsmag and is still selling stationery and newspapers.

West Street in about 1899. James Smith's butchers shop, established by 1899, is now Mick Starr's butchers and fishmongers, but the opposite corner has changed greatly. What is amazing is that this was the main road between Portsmouth and Chichester, and yet there are only two carts in sight!

West Street from the other end, and possibly the same day. Keppel Lodge is behind the trees on the left and the beautiful railings of the next house have disappeared. Also demolished are the houses on the right, which were replaced by a terrace of small Edwardian houses.

A terrace of houses in West Street: derelict by the early 1900s and ready for demolition. The three gentlemen would appear to be the owner of the demolition company, the foreman and the labourer. This is now the turning circle for the cul-de-sac that West Street has become.

Havant Road was an extension of West Street. On the left is Seafields House where Mr Kinnell lived. With his business partner, Mr Hartley, he established a large brewery in South Street in the late 1890s, which provided employment for Emsworth men until the late 1920s. The Emsworth Bowling Club had their green behind the King's Arms, and most matches were followed by a pint and a singsong around the piano kept in the bar.

Seafields House in 1852 was just to the west of the Emsworth Mill Pond, and is still there. Captain Henry Matson lived there at this time, followed by Mr Padwick and then Mr Noel Kinnell. He was a Councillor and a great benefactor of the town. It was a bequest in his will which enabled the promenade around the millpond to be levelled and surfaced. (Courtesy of Hampshire Library and Information Service)

It is many years since Cleveland Petrol was available. The house in the background is still recognisable today, but Payne's Garage, on the Havant Road, has altered drastically while between the two buildings is now Nore Farm Avenue.

This beautiful house was Nore Farm farmhouse on the road to Havant. It was bought by Mr Gibson and became the Brookfield Hotel in 1972. Now it is one of Emsworth's leading businesses and has expanded to include the house next door.

two

Through the Town: North to South

To the north of the town was the largest property in the area, Southleigh House. This was the home of Sir Woolmer White and his son, Sir Dymoke. The latter was very interested in coach driving and was seen regularly in Emsworth driving his coach and four. This photograph was taken in about 1900, and after they both died the house was closed and eventually sold as offices for a multinational company. (Courtesy of Hampshire Library and Information Service)

This photo of 1910 shows the lodge keeper's cottage of Southleigh House. These crossroads were known as Skull and Crossbones corner. It sounds very piratical, but may be a connection to the smuggling trade that was centred just north of here in Rowland's Castle. (Courtesy of Hampshire Library and Information Service)

En.th
(showing Junction of New Brighton and Horndean Roads)

This beautiful old house has long since disappeared from the junction of Horndean and New Brighton roads, and the junction has also altered. In 1910 the road to Horndean is on the left and New Brighton Road to Westbourne is the right. At one time it was hoped that Emsworth would rival Brighton as a bathing and seaside resort, but this was only a pipe dream. It remains only in the road name. (Courtesy of Hampshire Library and Information Service)

An easily recognised part of Emsworth, the southern entrance to the railway station in North Street in the early 1900s; the entrance to Sultan Road is the cobbled area to the right. The carters look as if they are waiting to load their goods on to the next train.

Looking in the opposite direction down North Street at the Railway Hotel on the corner of Sultan Road. Further down the road can be seen the side of The Locomotive, which was supplied by the local brewery, Kinnell & Hartley. This was demolished in the early 1960s and replaced by The Seagull. This was also demolished, in the 1990s, and the site is now a residential development.

Shops were not concentrated in one part of the town, but sprang up where there was a need. At the junction of Victoria Road and North Street, Mr. Harding poses outside his general store. Over the years, this shop was owned by Mr. Silk, as a butchers, Mr. Harding and Mr. January as general stores, and then an aquatic suppliers before reverting to residential use.

This dignified building is the Warblington UDC offices and fire station. The council chamber is on the top right, with the fire-engine garage through the arch below. Once the council no longer needed the building the hall was used for parties and dancing, because it has such a good dance floor. It is now the home of the Emsworth Museum.

The Little Green pub in North Street. It was sited where Tesco now is, and is remembered fondly as Dickie Bates' swap shop. As a pub it was first recorded in 1847 and closed in 1956. Mr Chitty was an early landlord who was also a local carrier.

The 1920s was a time when flying and photography combined. This photograph is one of a series of aerials of Emsworth taken in 1928, and this view shows St James' church surrounded by the graves of Emsworth worthies – and an exceedingly tall flag pole. The track along the bottom is now St James' Road, with the market gardens behind the North Street properties. North Street itself runs left to right through the middle of the picture, with Mr Silver's farm to the right, backing onto the fields leading down to the River Ems. The buildings opposite his farm were shops known as The Strand, and were reputedly decorated with columns from the portico of Stansted Park, which burnt down in 1904. The date does fit, and the columns are still there. To the left of the picture, opposite the open space, is the Milkman's Arms, one of Emsworth's defunct pubs, and beside it is another farm, which was used as a builder's yard for many years by Mr Rubick. In the bottom-right section is the new Parish Hall, built in 1924 together with the Church School. This was built with a schoolmaster's house attached, and the schoolmistress lived in the little cottage on the extreme right.

This is a very rare photograph of the junction of West Street, North Street and High Street. The row of buildings in the middle was demolished and a block of flats with shops beneath was constructed. Mr Agate's drapery shop on the left was opened before the beginning of the First World War, but had closed by the mid-1920s.

This depiction of Emsworth Square is possibly around 1840 as St Peter's Chapel became redundant when St James' church was built and consecrated. Many of the buildings are recognisable, although the Methodist church has not yet replaced Myrtle House on the left.

Emsworth Square in the late 1890s, still unpaved with one large light and a water pump. The Methodist Chapel was built in 1877 and St Peter's Chapel has now become the town hall.

A slightly idealised picture of Emsworth when the packman came with his haberdashery goods for the ladies to buy. The Swan pub was first recorded in 1833 and had stabling for seven horses. The house in the distance is Saffron House, which is now the Emsworth Bookshop.

Another early etching in idealised mood, with very small people, so the area looks much larger than it was, and is. The village pump has a light on top and seems enormous.

The area around the harbour at the bottom of South Street was the precarious world of the fishermen and their families. Their houses are smaller and poorer than those up the hill near the Square. The fisherman in the foreground is carrying a hand-dredge for dredging up oysters, which he would use while he was wading through the shallows.

Above: The quay and foreshore in 1961. If the planners had had their wish, by the end of the 1960s all of this area would have been a large marina covering the whole of Emsworth harbour, and the sea wall would have been the edge of a car park.

The mill at the bottom of South Street, which is now Emsworth Slipper Sailing Club. When it was built it had a major advantage over other mills in the area, in that sea-going vessels could moor against the mill wall and load directly from the mill, rather than having the cargo ferried out into the channel. The building was derelict by the 1960s and the sailing club persuaded Dittman & Malpas to sell the building to them. They then had the task of gutting the building and restoring it sympathetically. The only way to do so was to strip it out to the bare walls. When they lifted the floorboards there was a void filled with mud: it was felt that this should be removed, but after about 12ft they still had not got to the bottom, and the foundations of the walls were still going down. Therefore, they felt it was best to leave it as it was, and fill the void with rubble. This they obtained from the old shops in North Street which were being demolished to make way for the supermarket. There are not many places that can say that buildings in North Street are now in South Street.

Opposite below: This photograph was taken from 'The Banks' before it was resurfaced in the late 1920s. Everyone seems to have come out to see what the photographer was doing! The building to the left was the Anchor Inn, a one-time custom house. Behind it is the tall chimney of Kinnell & Hartley's Brewery.

A very tranquil view of Emsworth foreshore, taken from the bottom of King Street near J.D. Foster's boatyard at Hendy's Quay. In the distance, on the left, is the collection of buildings at the end of Bath Road, including the bathing house, now Emsworth Sailing Club. On the right are the buildings at the end of South Street, including the mill on the town quay; this became Emsworth Slipper Sailing Club.

This is the same day, but the photograph is taken further round on the Wadeway to Thorney Island. At one time the only access to the island was via the Wadeway at the bottom of King Street. The buildings on the extreme right are the industrial buildings in King Street, including the sail-making and rope-making works of Mr Lewis, formerly owned by his father–in–law, Mr Tatchell.

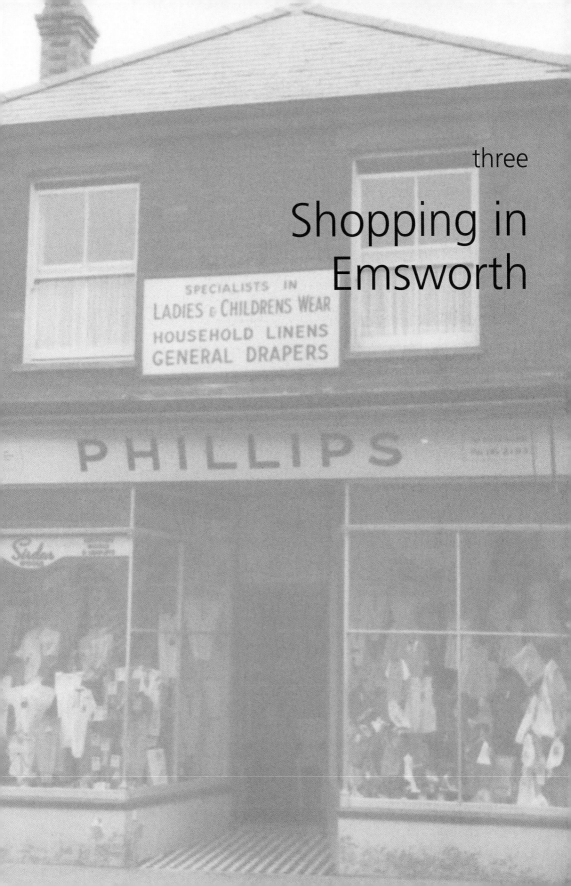

three

Shopping in Emsworth

SPECIALISTS IN
LADIES & CHILDRENS WEAR
HOUSEHOLD LINENS
GENERAL DRAPERS

PHILLIPS

This wonderful aerial photograph taken in the late 1920s shows the busy heart of the town from the south east. In the top left are the Victorian and Edwardian houses built along the road to Havant, with Beach Road stretching out left, and Emsworth House School opposite, where P.G. Wodehouse visited a friend in 1904, stayed ten years and used the village as a source of inspiration for many of his stories and characters. The fields in front are known as Seafields and have the old Coffin Path to Warblington crossing them diagonally. This path became known as Love Lane and then Warblington Road. Bath Road, beside the mill pond, is not yet complete and does not have the retaining sea wall. The top right corner shows the railway station, with a train leaving the station, while St James' church is in top middle surrounded by trees. Under the wing of the aircraft is the mill pond on the River Ems, serving the mill at the bottom of Queen Street, with its outfall into Dolphin Quay. Beside it is the large expanse of the Slipper Mill Pond, serving the Slipper Mill in the foreground. All around the mill are piles of logs used in shipbuilding, and the mill pond to the left is also used as a mast pond to season timber. This mill pond was originally constructed for another tide mill, but this never succeeded, and has now evolved into Emsworth Marina. All this wood was used by the shipbuilding company of J.D. Foster, which can be seen right in the middle of the picture, at the end of King Street. Not only were they shipbuilders, but also timber merchants, gravel merchants, fishermen and oyster merchants, so Mr Foster was one of the biggest employers in Emsworth. Moored out in the harbour are *Echo* and her sisters. These were the most advanced inshore fishing vessels of their time, with their raked prows making them fast through the water, and looking more like racing yachts than fishing boats. J.D. Foster designed them himself and each one was an evolution of the previous one. The final one came off the slipway in 1902, but was uncompleted because of the oyster pollution scare in that year. Oysters were stored in pens all along the harbour edge, and the sewer outfall was constructed to come out nearby. Unfortunately, one batch was unknowingly contaminated and sold for a banquet attended by many dignitaries in Winchester. Several of them were very ill, and the Dean of Winchester died, so a ban was placed on Emsworth oysters, which killed the trade dead. It never recovered. Thereafter, *Echo* and her sisters were more often in harbour than out.

At various times Emsworth has had many public houses: in fact, about twenty-five sites have been identified, and from the 1950s to the 1990s there were fourteen public houses, so pub crawls could take a long time. The Locomotive was in North Street until it was demolished to make way for The Seagull.

After the Second World War Hants & Sussex Motor Services started to run excursions to many different places. Their booking office was in North Street, just north of the junction with St James' Road. (Courtesy of Emsworth Museum)

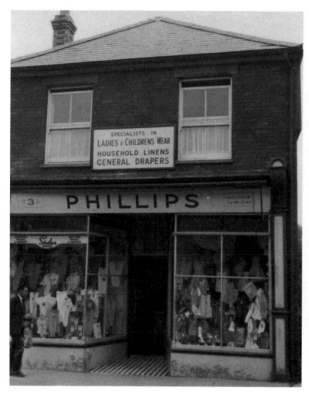

Left: One of the casualties of the short bypass, as the A259 was called, was Phillips. Miss Elizabeth Phillips started her millinery business in the early 1920s and by 1930 had developed into a drapery business. After the Second World War it was run by Mr Williams and sold clothing and household linen, as well as materials and patterns for dress making.

Below left: In 1911 Mr Hobson was the chemist in North Street, but by 1931 the owner was Cecil Williams, and he remained until the early 1960s, when Mr Yoward took it over. Here it is decorated for the Coronation of 1953.

Opposite above: Next door to the chemist was Fruits. Eric Lovell was based in Emsworth during the Second World War when he met Joy Whillier; they married and set up their fruit, vegetable and flower shop. It remained a feature of North Street until 1988, when Eric retired.

Opposite below: From the shadows this is a late afternoon. It may have been early closing day as there do not seem to be many customers. In June 1900 the shop keepers banded together to form a movement to promote earlier closing in Emsworth, and proposed suspending trading at 7.00 p.m. on Monday, Tuesday and Wednesday, and having an early closing day on Thursday, when they would close at 5.00 p.m.. This came into effect on 2 July 1900.

The grey building is the post office in the 1890s. Mrs Sarah Bell was postmistress and could deal with money orders, telegrams and parcel post with express delivery. Customers were assured that letters arrived from London and all parts, and were delivered at 7.00 a.m., 12.40 p.m. and 5.45 p.m. The Older Brothers were trading in Emsworth as grocers from the 1890s until after the First World War.

Fishing and oysters have always been essential to Emsworth, but photographs of them are rare. Here, Mrs House stands in the door of her shop next to the Black Dog in the Square, where she and her husband traded from the early 1900s to the mid-1930s, when they moved into High Street.

Birky Miller is seated in his favourite place on the Square with his pet heron and duck nearby. The Square is a lot more open than it is now, but even before the seated memorial was sited the local men all gathered there to yarn and pass the time of day. It was always the focal point of daily life in Emsworth.

From the 1930s, Jeram & Co. had been selling coal from their premises in the High Street, but here in the 1950s they are closed, along with Mr Davies, the gents' hairdresser. The site was derelict for many years, with proposals to move the post office there. However, this site is now Barclay's Bank.

A photograph of the 1920s showing W.E. Maidment trading at No. 4 High Street, in the same premises as the Older Brothers in the earlier photograph. He is a cycle salesman and repairer. Where the workmen are will eventually become the first site of Barclay's Bank.

J.R. Mant & Sons had seen a niche in the market here. Before the First World War they were already providing motor services, and who better to advertise than their other branch! The two vehicles are displayed outside their premises at the end of the High Street. Not only were they purveyors of meat, but they grazed their own cattle, possibly on the marshes around Thorney Island. By 1911 the motor services had taken over the whole premises and the butcher's shop had moved their business further along High Street.

Butchers were important in Emsworth, and H.H. Treagust is a family firm that are still trading in the same premises in the Square. This is a slightly later photograph from the 1930s, and the wonderful display could have been the celebration of the Silver Jubilee in 1935 or the Coronation in 1937.

The western side of the Square in the 1930s showing Pink's General Stores, the International Stores, the Methodist church and the Pavilion Cinema. This building was originally a chapel, then the town hall and in 1912 a cinema. It was in operation until the late 1950s and showed all the latest films. The listings were in the local paper and here they are advertising Harold Lloyd in *Movie Crazy*.

From before 1900, J. Young & Son was trading as a hairdresser and tobacconist at Nos 38 and 40 High Street. This photograph was taken in about 1925, showing a self-service machine outside the front of the shop. From the 1930s he was trading as a hairdresser only. The company was still trading in the same location in the 1950s. (Courtesy of Hampshire Library and Information Service)

The Anchor Inn right at the bottom of South Street seems to be a popular haunt with these fishermen. This would appear to be a Sunday because this was the only day they had time for standing and waiting, and is around 1899. The man in the white hat appears to have the name of his yacht on his jersey, which shows that he was a crewman on one of the pleasure yachts sailing and racing in the Solent. Many Emsworth fishermen were skilled enough to crew these big racing yachts during the summer months when the oyster trade was resting.

Mr Davis was the owner of two bakeries in Queen Street: one at the top of the hill and one here, opposite the Lord Raglan. This photo from about 1910 shows a thriving local business that catered for local customers in the town, but was able to make deliveries in the surrounding area. It looks like he collected the raw materials in the cart on the right, but made deliveries with the other three conveyances.

This engineering works was one of several in the town, and was in Palmers Road in the 1930s. It shows the men working in what we think of as primitive conditions, with very little lifting equipment, and no real working surfaces.

Lillywhite's Garage is still at the bottom of Queen Street. At the end of the Second World War the brothers bought the workshops and started their business. This photograph of 1962 shows the original garage. Just after this the major rebuilding work took place, and Davis' bakery was demolished to make way for the office area.

A few months later, the new office and store room has been built, and the workshop is being remodelled so that cars can pull in behind the pumps, allowing petrol to be dispensed from both sides at the same time.

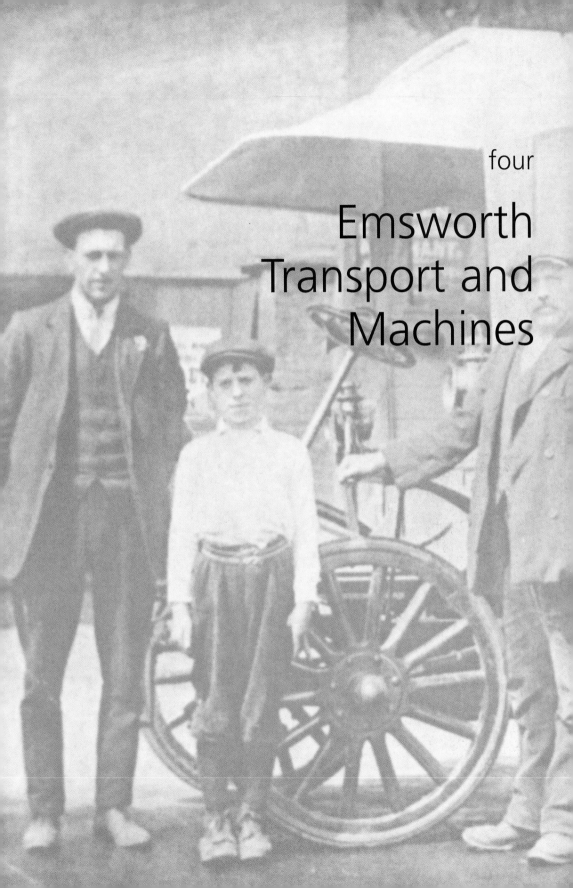

four

Emsworth Transport and Machines

Charabanc outings were very popular just after 1900, when people began to see the possibilities of outings, but did not have the means of getting there on their own. Here Mr Silver, holding the reins, is waiting in North Street to pick up his passengers.

Emsworth Mothers' Union organised outings for their members each year, and although they could not be termed 'Hen Nights', they were a means for members to have a few hours to themselves without having to look after their children. Here in 1904 the ladies are off on an outing from just outside the North Street entrance to St James' church.

A more modern charabanc taking the Mothers' Union on one of their outings in the early 1990s.

Another trip on a charabanc, but this time musical. This is an outing to the races from the Sussex Brewery in the early 1900s, and the lady in the background on the left is 'old' Mrs Miller, who was the publican's wife.

Many of the pubs in Emsworth arranged outings for their regulars. These very smart gents with their celebration cigars are boarding a charabanc outside the Milkman's Arms in North Street sometime during the 1930s.

George Newell, in the middle of the picture, ran his carrier's business from Marloe's House on the corner of Nile Street. He advertised daily deliveries and collections to and from Portsmouth.

George Newell now stands proudly by the driving seat of his lorry, having upgraded from horse and wagon. His eldest son, also George, aged twelve, is on the workforce in 1914. With so many men volunteering for war service, his help was needed.

This photograph from the late 1920s shows George Newell, Junior, leaning nonchalantly on the bonnet of his own vehicle. He went on to specialise in furniture removals and established his business in North Street.

This very faded photograph, taken before the First World War, shows J.D. Foster, in the white hat at the front, directing operations. It appears that they are clearing or cleaning out the slipway at Hendy's Quay. (Courtesy of Hampshire Library and Information Service)

Not only did J.D. Foster need timber for his shipbuilding activities, he exported it all over the British Empire. This enormous traction engine was used to bring tree trunks from the woods to the north of Emsworth for storage in various sites around the area. The stack in Bridge Road was not removed until the late 1960s.

J.D. Foster's men used many forms of transport. This photograph was taken at the junction of King Street and Stanley Road, and shows the cradle used to transport large tree trunks. The cradle would be positioned over the logs, lowered so the logs could be chained to it, and then lifted and attached to the lorry.

This photograph of J.D. Foster's workshop shows one of his traction engines being used as a stationery engine, extending its life. There were many processes that needed more than manpower and the traction engine is being used to power the circular saw, which looks very hazardous in the foreground.

J.D. Foster was an enthusiastic cyclist all his life, and was a prominent member of the Emsworth Cycling Club. He also used his bicycle as his everyday transport. Here he is cycling out of his yard on his eightieth birthday.

Kinnell & Hartley's brewery in South Street was a large employer of men from the late 1890s until the late 1920s. Here the traction engine team is delivering essential supplies to the George Inn in North Street, Havant.

Mr Horrocks is seen here outside his hardware shop in the High Street with his Rolls Royce. He traded from just after the First World War until the premises were destroyed by fire in 1960. Did he not have a delivery van? It does seem sacrilegious to use a Rolls Royce to deliver fencing for a customer.

Mr Lewis worked for J.D. Foster, but during his spare time he was a Scout leader, and his Austin 7 was ideal transport for him and his kit bag.

Delivery boys on bicycles are part of the history of shopping, and here in the late 1940s Fruits in North Street employed their own delivery boy. He is photographed in North Street, on the other side of the road from the shop.

Later Fruits were able to upgrade to a delivery van, and here Eric Lovell poses proudly beside his vehicle. The telephone number is interesting: Emsworth 17.

Hants & Sussex Motor Services ran the route from Emsworth station to Thorney Island. It started just before the Second World War, and here a large detachment of WAAFs are being embarked for the trip. This was not a rare occurrence, and without this bus route the armed services would have had to deploy large numbers of lorries for transport purposes.

After the Second World War Hants & Sussex Motor Services expanded in the civilian routes. Here the new housing estate at the end of Victoria Road finally gets its own bus service. It was a long way to walk from the top of Victoria Road into town, and with young children it could take a long time, so the bus service was opened in 1949.

Taking advantage of Emsworth on a very quiet Sunday morning, Eric Lovell and Fred Somerill exercise their horses in North Street in the 1960s. The shop on the left was a delicatessen owned by Mrs Whillier, with her fishmonger's shop the next one down with the sunblind.

This beautiful pair of greys, steaming in a cold winter morning, belonged to HM the Queen, and were a present from Germany. They were sent to Sir Dymoke White for schooling to pull carriages, and were trained by his coachman, Arthur Showell, who is seen here holding the reins. After Sir Dymoke's death, Mr Showell became head coachman to the Queen.

five

Fishing and the Sea in Emsworth

Emsworth Harbour in the early 1960s, and the final days of J.D. Foster's wonderful fleet of oyster smacks. Five of them lie rotting in the mud along with the Ark, which is the square structure to the left of the picture. A challenge for boys and swimmers for nearly 100 years, the Ark was a well known feature of Emsworth Harbour. It was in position just off the main channel in the Harbour by 1898, but removed in 1978. It was built of pine and was 100ft long, 50ft wide and 25ft high, weighing about 3,000 tons and was reputed to have cost J.D. Foster £2,000 to build. J.D. Foster designed it as a landing stage for his oyster smacks, and the lower half was a storage tank for scallops. There were two sluices to control the flow of water to ensure that the scallops did not dry out at low tide, but the water could flow through to keep it fresh at high tide. The project was not a success, because the scallops did not thrive, and it was thought that this was because the Ark had been covered in tar to preserve it. It had been built on the ramps at Hendy's Quay and launched on the spring tide, with its sluices closed, so that it could be floated into position. Then the sluices were opened and it was fixed into position with chains. At the launching there was such a wash set up when it hit the water that it is said that small boats moored near Slipper Mill were capsized, and J.D. Foster received several complaints. Emsworth Harbour was declared contaminated in 1903, so the Ark was redundant, and then the First World War prevented a renewal of the oyster trade in any quantity, so it was not used for its original purpose after its first few years. Instead it was a mooring for the large oyster smacks and a target for adventurous youngsters. Its last useful purpose was as a platform for the firework display that ended the celebrations to mark the Silver Jubilee of Queen Elizabeth II in 1977.

This photograph was taken a few years earlier, possibly the early 1950s, when the oyster fleet was still upright in the water. In the foreground can be seen the remains of the oyster pens, which were holes dug into the mud of the foreshore, supported by planking and timber so they did not cave in. They were used to store the oysters until they were needed. Because the pens were below the high water mark they would be flushed with clean water twice a day, which cleaned the oysters and kept them fresh.

Most people remember the Ark as a wreck, but here its true size can be appreciated. This photograph was taken during the Ark's construction in 1896 or 1897 from near Slipper Mill and it shows the workforce dwarfed by it. How J.D. Foster could conceive of launching her from this site is amazing, but she was launched and towed into position, where she remained until 1978.

Anyone who has lived in Emsworth for a while will be aware of *Echo*. She was the last fully working oyster smack built by J.D. Foster. He was renowned for building working vessels that looked like racing yachts, and this photograph shows her lines well. She was the only one to be steam powered, although her sister ships had steam winches. J.D. Foster built her in 1900 and she was registered in March 1901, so was only in use for 18 months before disaster struck Emsworth's oysters. The crew could number up to eleven and she would be at sea for several weeks searching and dredging for oysters. After the pollution problems in Emsworth Harbour in 1902 she tended to be based at Newhaven, where the oysters could be taken by train directly to London. The crew, however, were still living in Emsworth and had to make their own way home at the end of each voyage. If the catch had been poor, they did not receive much money, and they would have to walk home. They had been known to sing in pubs and chapels on their way to earn enough money to eat (and drink?). Many Emsworth fishermen are recorded in the registers as being on the crew at some time. J.D. Foster would promote them up through the boats as they got more experienced. They would start on the older ones and work their way up, so if they were appointed to serve on *Echo* everyone knew that they were experienced and trusted oyster fishermen.

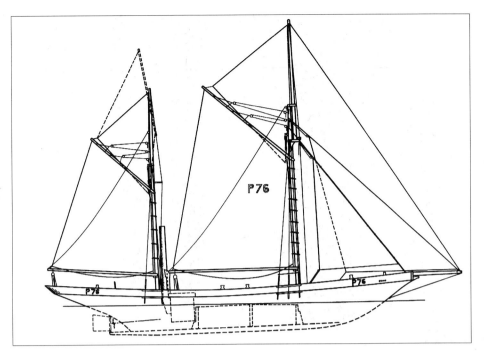

A line drawing for *Echo* showing her sail plan. Also shown are the two large tanks where the oysters were stored. In order to keep them fresh after they had been dredged, the oysters were put into these tanks, and sea water was pumped through them. The oysters would use this water and would therefore clean themselves of all the sand and grit from the sea floor.

An early photo from the 1890s showing Emsworth at high tide. There does not seem to be much activity in the harbour, so this could be during the main oyster season, which ran from September to April each year. During the season, J.D. Foster, who had the largest business in Emsworth at this time, was selling about £3 million-worth of oysters a year to towns and cities all over the south coast, including large quantities to London. (Courtesy of Hampshire Library and Information Service)

Terror was one of the small boats built to work in the harbour. When the oyster trade suffered its severe decline in the early 1900s she was used for trips and outings. This photograph shows her embarking day trippers from Hayling Beach.

Grampus was the sister of *Terror*, and was built in about 1898 by J.D. Foster and owned by Jack Kennett. She moved oysters from the pens at Mill Rythe, Hayling Island, up to the holding pens near South Street.

1912 and all seems quiet in the harbour. All the large oyster smacks were operating out of Newhaven, so this lone fisherman has the harbour to himself, although the workmen at the mill are busy unloading. (Courtesy of Hampshire Library and Information Service)

This fishing boat of the early 1960s is still following the traditions of the earlier fishermen. Here the boat is so shallow-drafted that it is able to pull up on the shore without any danger of being stuck. The skipper, on the left, is one of the Treagust family, who have been fishing for several generations.

Thorney Island, seen here in Portsmouth Harbour, was built by William Foster in Emsworth in 1871. William was the father of J.D. Foster, and his shipyard was situated further up King Street. *Thorney Island*, at 184 tons, was the largest vessel built in Emsworth, and was used to carry gravel and ballast from Langstone and Chichester harbours up to Newcastle, returning with coal. She was also known to trade with Russia via the White Sea. After being dismantled for use as a hulk in 1897, she was broken up in 1917.

Possibly the sister ship of *Thorney Island*, *Sarah Amy*, or *Sarah King* as she was registered, was also built by William Foster in 1865. She was built for Cox of Portsmouth, who were coal merchants, and was used to transport coal and clay between the ports of north east England and Portsmouth.

Sylvia was designed and built by J.D. Foster in 1896. She was one of the earlier oyster smacks that he used to dredge for oysters in the English Channel. Although the oyster pollution scare of 1902 caused the inshore market to collapse, the larger smacks would travel along the Channel as far as Falmouth and across to the French Coast. An experienced skipper learnt where to find the best hauls. In 1927 *Sylvia*'s skipper was John Parham, a very experienced fisherman who had worked for J.D. Foster for over thirty years and lived in South Street. His father had also been employed by the Foster family for many years. The crew were Cecil Hancock, Percy Middleton, Edwin Noyce, Charlie Burton and Albert Hazell. She left Emsworth at the end of October, but no one knew definitely when she would return, because it depended upon how successful they were. Mrs Parham received a postcard from her husband from Le Havre dated in the middle of November saying that they were on their way back, but they were never heard of again. On 29 November a steamer, *Clyde Rock*, reported a collision with a schooner forty miles south of St Catherine's Point, Isle of Wight. The other vessel sank immediately and although the captain of *Clyde Rock* ordered a search lasting several hours, no wreckage or survivors were found. This was not the first oyster smack lost in this way. *Sylvia*'s sister ship *Una* had been lost in December 1906 in similar circumstances. The local newspaper reported the tragedy widely and commented that it seems so much worse when it happens just before Christmas. A fund was set up in Emsworth immediately to provide relief for the families, and the memorial service held in St James' church was very well attended.

This photograph of the early 1920s encapsulates Emsworth's fishing industry. In the foreground is a wildfowling punt, which was used in the harbour to control the duck and geese, as well as providing meat for the table. The larger vessel in the foreground is *Grampus*, owned by Mr Jack Kennett, originally to ferry oysters around the harbour, and later to give boat trips in the harbour and off the beaches at Hayling Island. Also visible is the massive bulk of the Ark, looking derelict, but an ideal pontoon for the oyster fleet. The oyster smacks of J.D. Foster can be seen moored in the channel leading to his shipyard at Hendy's Quay. They were built in the 1890s and were the most advanced inshore fishing vessels built in Britain at that time, and were more like racing yachts than working boats. They all had 'J.D.F.' on the transom at the stern and were lime-washed to protect the wood. Most of them were crewed by four to six men, although *Echo*, which was the last and therefore most advanced, was steam driven and had between eight and eleven crew. Most of them were used to dredge oysters from the English Channel from France to Falmouth. When the industry was destroyed by the pollution of Emsworth's foreshore in 1902, they sailed out of Newhaven. Between *Grampus* and the oyster fleet, sticking out of the mud, can be seen the remains of the oyster pens. These pens were dug out of the mud and lined with timber; at high tide they were covered with water and would be freshened on each tide, in order to keep the dredged oysters fresh until they were needed for market. When the oyster industry failed they were left to decay and fill with mud, so that only the timber shows their outlines.

Above: Echo in her last days was moored at the end of Hendy's Quay. Here she is with her funnel broken through decay, and J.D. Foster's shipyard deserted and derelict.

Right: A last photograph of *Echo*, showing her waiting for demolition, yet still proudly carrying 'J.D.F.' on her transom. In the background one of her sister ships is laying near the channel awaiting the same fate. The shipyard is being destroyed and the site is now housing. *Echo* was broken up on 28 November, 1962.

The launching of *Windflower* from Mr Kemp's yard in Emsworth was a big occasion. It was the first large vessel to be launched since the slump of 1902, and Dr French, the owner, entertained forty guests to lunch at the Crown Hotel, and provided refreshments for all the shipyard employees and their lady friends in a separate room. Dr French was also King George V's personal physician. The doctor loved the danger of sailing in bad weather and on many occasions the crew had concerns about getting safely into port. William Prior was the skipper of *Windflower* and worked for Dr French for many years. After one notable occasion, when William had serious difficulty bring the yacht back into harbour, he wrote to Dr French handing in his notice. He did not get a reply for six weeks, when Dr French arrived in his chauffeur-driven car with a large oil painting of *Windflower*, and a request for William to remain his skipper. The painting is still in the possession of the Prior family.

Opposite above: Another of the beautiful oyster smacks, *Nonpareil*, has been dragged from her mooring in the main channel by the storm of 1934 and beached along the foreshore. The logs were used to assist with mooring the oyster smacks out in the harbour, but the force of the storm had dragged them up together with the smacks.

Opposite below: This sad photograph of 1967 shows *Nonpareil* as she breaks up in the harbour. Where she was covered by the tide, her port side is covered with seaweed, and on the starboard side the decking is about to collapse. The mounting for the steam winch, for hauling in the oyster dredges, can be seen towards the bow. Within a few years there was nothing left of this beautiful vessel.

It was not just working boats that were built in Emsworth. Pleasure craft of all sizes began their lives here. This vessel is possibly *Spitfire*, built for Lord Mountbatten. He lived at Asdean, just north of Emsworth, while serving in the Navy at Portsmouth and in 1931/32 he was Commodore of Emsworth Sailing Club.

Oyster fishing was only possible during the winter months, so the oyster fishermen either returned to their smaller fishing boats during the summer or they joined the crews of the large sailing yachts that were racing out of Cowes. Sir Thomas Lipton and King George V were two of the owners. Here the crew of White Heather pose in 1922. They include Jim Parham, Will Boutell, Charlie Burton and Arthur Dridge.

A rather bleak water photograph showing the oyster smacks moored against the Ark. In the middle is the tall chimney of Mr Foster's ship yard in King Street and to the left the chimney of the saw mill. In the shipyard between, a yacht is nearing completion.

This view of Emsworth from the bottom of Bath Road was taken before 1928 and shows the chimney of Kinnell & Hartley's brewery on the left and the mill at the town quay in the middle. In the foreground is the mill pond, which has been staked to support eel traps.

After the pollution of the oyster beds and subsequent decline of the industry, J.D. Foster expanded his business into other forms of shipbuilding and fitting out. Here he is (left) in the 1930s, supervising the installation of a large diesel engine into a vessel moored at Hendy's Quay.

J.D. Foster's expertise in building ships led to various other activities. Here the 'men from the ministry' are standing on a platform that was designed to test the water resistance of paints used on ships. The platform was moored in Dolphin Quay, painted with various substances and left to weather.

Fishing is a cold business and even in winter there is work to be done. This photograph from before the First World War shows the sea freezing, but the men still had to repair their nets and make repairs to the boats so that they were ready to go fishing.

Emsworth may be in a sheltered harbour, but it can still get extremes of weather. 1963 was one of the coldest winters for many years with people skating on the mill ponds, and the sea water frozen over much of the harbour area. This photograph shows the swans swimming on one of the small areas of clear water, but even Emsworthian fishermen are staying at home.

A very bleak picture of a run-down harbour in the 1950s. During the Second World War there had been a ban on fishing outside the harbour, and it was not really very safe along the south coast. The oyster industry was unregulated and whenever the Dredgermens' Association tried to regenerate the industry something happened to prevent them: either the oysters were destroyed by yacht moorings or someone poached them. The old Anchor Inn stands virtually derelict, where once it had served as a customs point for the harbour. It was soon to be leased by the Emsworth Slipper Sailing Club, who would then purchase the mill nearby, leaving the property to become a restaurant. The fishermen's houses in South Street were being condemned as unfit to live in, and they were moving to other parts of Emsworth. Soon, however, the picture would change; the properties would be restored and used as holiday homes and retirement homes, and the whole area would become as charming and picturesque as it is now.

six

Events (Good and Bad) in Emsworth

Above: Another view of the storm damage in the harbour in 1934, with the locals out checking on their vessels and those of their neighbours. The severity of the storm can be gauged by the size of the vessels moved when compared with the people. This is near the end of Stanley Road.

Left: The 1930s seem to have had some very cold winters. This photograph, taken from the bottom of School Lane, shows the mill pond frozen, and the village youths playing ice hockey. The depth of ice can be seen by the amount that has been disturbed around the children at the front.

Opposite below: Funerals were a way of showing public appreciation for local people. Here, in North Street on 12 October 1912, is the funeral of Harry Louch, who had been a fireman for many years and died after a long illness. At the top of the photograph can just be seen the fire engine carrying the coffin, and in front are firemen from Emsworth joined by contingents from Fareham, Havant and Portsmouth.

Above: Even into the 1980s the winter could produce some very cold snaps. Here Slipper Pond has been frozen enough for children to enjoy skating and tobogganing. The masts are yachts moored in Dolphin Quay, which tended to remain free of ice due to the faster flowing water.

For many years the residents of Emsworth had thanked the Emsworth firemen for their commitment with an annual dinner held in the British Legion Hall. In April 1962, the firemen were very disappointed that they were not able to save the wooden hall from a devastating fire, which destroyed it completely. Bill Griffin, the senior fire officer, can be seen running towards the camera.

Another devastating fire occurred in September 1960, when Horrock's the ironmongers, in High Street, was destroyed. Not only was it a very old building, but there were many inflammable substances inside. Behind was Beta Marine, which manufactured fibreglass boats: it was also destroyed. The fire brigade had a hard task preventing the fire from spreading to adjoining buildings.

After the First World War the returning servicemen endowed a bed in the hospital as a memorial to their fallen comrades. In a similar manner, after the Second World War they did not want a lump of stone as a memorial; they wanted something of use to their community as a mark of respect. In December 1950 they and all their families gathered in the Square to dedicate the covered memorial seating, near the bus stop. (Courtesy of Emsworth Museum)

Remembrance Day has always been an important occasion in Emsworth, and all the youth organisations parade through the town as a mark of respect. Usually, they were led by T.S. Unity, the local Nautical Training ship, and here the Boys' Brigade, Girl Guides and Girls' Brigade are waiting to form up.

Above: Confirmation into the Church of England was a big occasion for many people. Here Revd Douglas Caiger, on the left, poses with his latest group in the mid-1960s, together with the Bishop of Portsmouth.

Above: A group of parents waiting to be entertained at the fair at Emsworth School in Washington Road. It is 1913 and no respectable person would be seen without a hat!

Right: These gentlemen appear to have had a good time at the Emsworth Sports Day in 1913. Emsworth may be a small town, but they were up-to-date with national events. The suffragettes have their supporters, but the group on the right looks more like the Mafia.

Opposite below: The procession of boats drifting down the harbour on the tide, resting on the gravel banks, which shifted with the tides, and collecting gravel, which would be used as ballast in cargo vessels and traded for coal and other goods, was a daily event. The gravel was collected by running a wheelbarrow down a ramp onto the bank, filling it by hand, and then running back up the ramp. As the tide came in, flooding the banks, the boats would drift back up the harbour to discharge their cargo on the quay.

EMSWORTH SPORTS 1913
THE POLICEMAN AND THE
SUFFRAGETTES

This may not have been the Olympics, but this sports event in about 1908 has attracted a big crowd. Emsworth Cycle Club was very popular for many years.

When they were not fighting fires, Emsworth's firemen were busy enjoying themselves. Here they are at the annual national union week at Tonbridge in 1909, and obviously entertaining the other groups.

In 1975 St James' Church School finally proved too old and small for the modern needs, and a new building was erected in Bellevue Lane. All the present and past pupils marked the occasion by processing in Victorian costume from the old to the new. A few years later the building was gutted by fire, but again it was rebuilt and goes from strength to strength.

The school hall in the new St James' School was used for many purposes and during the 1980s was used extensively for school productions. Here, *O Hara San* is playing to a packed audience of devoted parents and grandparents.

Above: This is possibly another Empire Day during the 1920s, with lots of small children assembled in the grounds of Emsworth School. In the background is the signal box at the western end of Emsworth station.

Right: A more mechanised procession passing along High Street, led by the Emsworth fire brigade in all their glory.

Opposite above: When St James' School no longer needed their old premises there was great debate about the future use of the building. Eventually a group of residents formed the Emsworth Community Association to run the building as a community centre. As funds allowed the old building was revamped and added to. In the late 1980s funds became available to build an extension. This is called the Lumley Room and was opened by the actress Joanna Lumley.

Opposite below: Carnivals and processions were regular events in Emsworth and here the procession is about the pass under the railway bridge, heading into Emsworth. From the patriotic decorations it would appear to be Empire Day in the 1920s.

Above: Emsworth used to have a festival week in August, and one day in the week would be the Water Carnival. Anything that could float was put into the mill pond. At this time there were sluice gates that could be opened at high tide near the mill, so all the vessels could be floated into the mill pond. Saturday 29 August 1953 was the day set aside in Emsworth to mark the Queen's Coronation. There was a fifty-page souvenir programme available and admission to the arena was one shilling for adults and sixpence for children. Seating had been arranged around the mill pond, which people could book. The main grandstand was seven shillings and sixpence, but some of the less favoured seats could be purchased for three shillings. It was stated in the programme that all seats were bookable in advance, and there would be no refunds. The map in the centre showed the first aid points, refreshments, seating areas and directions to the car parks. In fact over 1,000 cars descended on Emsworth, which must have been a strain for the local police force. There were frogmen, a floating bandstand, a trip to the pirates cave, model powerboat demonstrations and illuminated fountains. The parade and judging of boats was at 4.00 p.m., but from 11.00 a.m. there was constant entertainment. Here, in the parade of boats, the sheik is being towed by his harem. Apparently it was such hard work that they fell behind in the procession and had to have a tow from a motorised friend. The float at the front sank, and the boat at the back was swamped. A good time was had by all!

Opposite above: Another entry in the Water Carnival. From the amount of activity on the boats it would appear that this is the lull between rehearsal and the evening performance – or the pubs had just opened!

Opposite below: This evening picture of the water carnival, taken along Bridgefoot Path, shows the anticipation of the audience waiting for the procession. The lights in the distance are strings along the promenade. No worries about health and safety here, because the mums will scoop the children out of the water if they fall in.

There were many organisations in Emsworth that indulged in amateur dramatic productions: the Mothers' Union produced *Pride and Prejudice* in 1961.

The Emsworth Brotherhood started as a club for men to improve their minds with discussions and debates. Here they were improving their bodies as well by winning a trophy for their proficiency in the 1932/3 football season.

Another popular organisation was the Royal Antediluvian Order of Buffalos, which had an active group of members. Here they pose for a photograph in the late 1940s.

The church hall was the scene for many parties for all age groups. The Young Wives' Club was a junior branch of Mothers' Union, and held Christmas parties for their children here. They were at their strongest during the 1960s.

These children are celebrating the Coronation of George V in 1911. Behind them can be seen the Ship Inn and, further to the left, Mr Horrock's hardware shop and then the Crown Hotel.

Another royal occasion was marked by the traders in North Street. This time it was Queen Elizabeth II's Silver Jubilee in 1977. All the shops had been decorated for the occasion, and after closing time they had a big street party.

seven

Institutions in Emsworth

St James' church in 1917. Because this photograph was taken before the end of the First World War, there are no memorials to the fallen in the sanctuary. The font is just in the bottom of the picture, so it is still in its traditional position inside the west door. In 1921 a baptistery was erected in the north-west corner in memory of Jessie Robinson.

This later photograph was taken in the late 1990s and shows that the altar has now been moved into the body of the church, while the original altar at the eastern end is surrounded by wooden panels inscribed with the names of Emsworth people who died during (and since) the two world wars.

This photograph is of the first Baptist church to be built in Emsworth in 1808, which was replaced in the 1890s by a bigger establishment on the same site. At that time it had its own graveyard, but all burials were transferred to the municipal cemetery at Warblington, and therefore there was also room to build a church hall.

The Emsworth Mothers' Union was one of the first Unions to be formed in 1880 or 1882. Here they pose for a group photograph in the garden of the Rectory in Havant Road in the late 1940s.

Emsworth Parish Hall, which used to be called St James' Church Hall, has been home to many organisations that have used it for all sorts of events. Here the Emsworth Young Wives' Club are performing one of their fund-raising revues in the 1960s.

Meetings of all sorts took place, and still take place, in the Parish Hall. In the 1960s the Mothers' Union assembled regularly to listen to speakers and to exchange gossip and information over a cup of tea.

As the term implies, Mothers' Union members were mothers, and their children were enrolled in the Children's Union. This was a very active group during the 1950s and 1960s and here a group of them pose on the stage of the Parish Hall.

The Emsworth fire brigade have attended many fires in their history. Here in 1911 they are practicing near the pond at Lumley Mill. It took about six or seven minutes for the boiler to build steam, and the driver tried to time their arrival at the fire so the boiler was ready to pump water immediately. (Courtesy of Hampshire Library and Information Service)

This early formal photograph of about 1885 shows the Emsworth fire brigade in their uniforms, complete with brass helmets. This was before the telephone could be used to call the men, so the bugler, on the right of the picture, would have to run to four points in the town and blow the warning that the firemen were needed. (Courtesy of Hampshire Library and Information Service)

This later formal photograph, taken in 1939, is posed in front of the fire station. Within a short time many of these men were helping to quench the flames of the Blitz in Portsmouth during the Second World War. (Courtesy of Hampshire Library and Information Service)

Emsworth is situated on the south coast, and so the residents have always been keen to do their bit to protect their homes and country. This photograph shows a very smart Emsworth Home Guard – nothing like the incompetent 'Dad's Army' we are led to believe they were.

The primary school in Emsworth was known as the Council School, and was built on the site in Washington Road in 1909. Here the buildings, nearing completion, are being built by Frank Privett (builders). The caption on this photograph refers to schools, so it was obviously boys and girls in separate sections.

This photograph of a class at the Washington Road school was taken during the First World War, and the boy in the front seems to be holding a shield. He also appears to be wearing Boy Scout uniform.

Emsworth Primary School stayed in Washington Road until the late 1990s. By this time it was the infant section only, with the junior section moving to a new building further up Victoria Road in the 1970s. Here the senior class in 1957/58 pose outside the bike shed for their annual photograph. Many of these youngsters went on to Warblington Secondary School.

St James' Church School was formerly the National School, based in Bridgefoot Path, but moved into the building near St James' church in the 1870s. Here the senior class in 1960/61 is photographed at the top of Church Path, where the hedge divides the road from the churchyard. The teacher on the right is Monty Reed, who taught many children in Emsworth and Havant over the years. He was well liked and is still fondly remembered.

St James' Church School became too big for the site near the church and moved to Bellevue Lane in 1974, and the old school building became the community centre. This photograph of the senior class of 1983/84 contains the children of the many of the pupils in the previous photograph.

Above: Music played an important part in many people's lives, especially if they were connected with a church. Here the Primitive Methodist Band poses for the photographer in 1910. The church is still on the Square and many of the families of these men still live in Emsworth.

Left: This group of Emsworth lads met together regularly to go swimming and compete against other local groups. Here they are posing at Northney in 1954.

Opposite below: Although Emsworth's Scout troop were active from the early 1920s it was not until later that they purchased their campsite at South Harting. It was the base for many outdoor activities and camps. The Beavers, seen here in the 1950s, could have been camping there.

Above: Boy Scouts and Girl Guides have been active in Emsworth since the 1920s, but to be photographed together then is quite rare. Both associations have strong units still in Emsworth.

Girl Guides have been an important part of Emsworth since the 1920s and here Eunice Sanderson, on the left, is taking them to camp in the 1950s. They loaded up their kit in the Congregational church gardens, and the Jersey Dairy can just be seen on the left.

The highest award a Girl Guide can work towards is her Queen's Guide. Here Guides from 2nd Emsworth and 3rd Emsworth Guide Companies are receiving their award from Mary Dymott, the District Commissioner for Emsworth, in 1988.

The Boys' Brigade had been active in Emsworth for many years, and was attached to the Baptist church. In 1989 they moved into the Parish Hall, and became affiliated to the Church of England. This photograph shows them with the Bishop of Portsmouth in St James' church after the dedication service.

Here a group of Boys' Brigade members pose in the Parish Hall after their awards presentation evening. Two of the lads achieved the highest award for the Boys' Brigade and were invited to parade before HM the Queen at Windsor Castle.

One of the younger uniformed groups to be part of Emsworth was the Nautical Training Corps. They formed their own marching band which led youth parades and processions for some years. Here T.S. Unity are leading the parade along Bridge Road.

The Emsworth Red Cross turned out in force in December 1946 to mark the retirement of Mrs Soames as Commandant of the Emsworth Detachment. They had a presentation at Southleigh House followed by tea.

The St John's Ambulance Brigade is another uniformed organisation that has been prominent in Emsworth for many years, providing first aid cover for many of the events. Here they are at the official opening of their new headquarters building in Convent Lane.

Sport is always important in a community and here the Emsworth Wednesday Football Club of 1913 pose for their team photograph.

The next generation of Emsworth Wednesday pose for their team photograph. From the state of the ground it would appear to be the end of the season in 1927, rather than the beginning in 1926.

Slightly later, the football club has grown, and the team photograph shows a considerably wider age range. This is possibly from the 1930s.

The Emsworth United football team of 1947/48 have done themselves proud with a selection of cups and a shield.

Not only football but hockey was popular in Emsworth, and here the team pose in the 1930s. However, the whole team does not seem to be present on this day.

Over its long life, since 1919 when it was formed, Emsworth Horticultural Show has been held at different times and in different places. For many years it was an inside show for produce and flowers. For the last few years it has been held on the Emsworth Recreation Ground, with a giant marquee to hold the hundreds of exhibits that are entered. Competition is always fierce but friendly. The competition is now open to handicrafts and children, as well as the traditional classes of fruit and vegetables. Judging is performed by national judges and the standard is always high. Exhibits are also sold at the end of the show, and there is no shortage of buyers. Outside the marquee there are a wide range of stalls offering goods for sale, and many Emsworth organisations take the opportunity to recruit new members or to show off their achievements and aims. The arena provides entertainment for the family all afternoon with bands, dog training and other interesting events. The Mayor of Havant is usually invited to open it, and in 1985 an Emsworth Councillor was Mayor, so Mrs Tessa Daines was especially pleased to perform the ceremony.

Opposite above: The darts team of the Bluebell Inn, in South Street, seem to have had a particularly successful season. This photograph is from the 1950s.

Opposite below: Emsworth Horticultural Show is one of the main events of village life and at this early show in the 1950s, the judges are inspecting some of the flower entries. Here the show is being held in the British Legion Hall, which was behind the Baptist church in North Street.

In 1999 it was recognised that independent traders in Emsworth were struggling for business and having to compete with the out-of-town supermarkets. The business association proposed that, as Emsworth had a preponderance of eating-out establishments, and a large proportion of food retailers, a celebration of their trade should be arranged. That was the beginning of the Emsworth Food Festival, which was first held in 2001. In the first year it attracted 8,000 people, but it also caught the imagination of the community and it has grown over the years, so that it now takes over the whole area for three days in September and attracts many thousands of visitors. Many of these visitors are impressed enough to return at other times of the year, and since the inception of the Festival the business community has grown in confidence. For three days Emsworth enjoys eating, drinking and all the free entertainment that is on offer in various places. The other benefit is that all profits from the event are put straight back into community projects.

eight

Notable
Emsworthians

Above: Mr Silver (with his hand on his horse) owned the farm across the road from the fire station in North Street. When the alarm sounded Mr Silver allowed his son to take the farm horses across the road to pull the fire engine to the fire. If the horses were in use on the farm, the fire engine had to wait until they could be brought in from the fields. (Courtesy of Hampshire Library and Information Service)

Opposite below: Miss Isobel Silver, daughter of Mr Silver, became a local celebrity when she took her brother's place to drive the fire engine when Blendworth Hall was destroyed by fire in 1917. The fact a lady had driven a fire engine was recorded in several national newspapers. (Courtesy of Hampshire Library and Information Service)

Right: Harry Louch was a respected resident of Emsworth, who died aged seventy-five years in 1912. He lived in Victoria Road and had his own building and house decorating business. Also he was senior fireman with the Emsworth fire brigade.

Below: Bill Griffin was the grandson of Harry Louch and followed his grandfather and father into the decorating business, as well as being a fireman. Whilst Senior Fire Officer he trained his brigade to a very high standard, so that they won the county competition thirteen years out of fifteen. He felt that if they were well trained in competitions, they would be able to work instinctively at a fire. He died aged ninety-one in 2006, while attempting a new dance at his dancing club.

Wyndham Miller was the idiosyncratic landlord of the Sussex Brewery until the early 1970s. He was the last of a family brewing business going back to 1860. Although he said he did not gamble, he never missed a meeting at Fontwell or Goodwood, and very often closed the pub to attend. Here he is standing at the back of the pub with a large punt gun used in wildfowling.

Basil Williams started his bus company at the age of twenty-two in 1937, becoming the youngest transport operator in the country, with the aim of serving the new RAF base at Thorney Island. This route was maintained all through the Second World War, as well as contracts to transport many essential workers to and from their places of work all over the south coast. The bus depot was a small workshop in Sultan Road, with the office above. After the war he opened a bus service to the new Victoria Road houses, and a booking office in North Street. He lived at Hollybank House for some years, and was involved in the Men of Trees and other conservation bodies.

James Duncan Foster, photographed leaning nonchalantly against a wall on his eightieth birthday. It is believed that he rode to the New Forest and back on this day. He was born in 1858 in King Street, the third son of William Foster, and he lived all his life in Emsworth, dying in 1940. His thriving oyster and scallop business was started in 1895 and he increased his trade by buying out those in Emsworth who wished to sell their oyster beds. He built his first oyster smack in 1889, and they all had 'J.D.F.' painted on the transom in black. He was one of the main architects of Emsworth as it is today with his energy and drive to build and develop his fishing fleet, and in 1927 was listed as timber merchant, shipbuilder and owner, sail maker, oyster merchant, farmer, traction engine proprietor and haulage contractor, and gravel and sand contractor for the Admiralty. He must have employed more people in Emsworth than anyone else, and therefore his influence was vast, and he left the legacy of a fleet of the most advanced inshore fishing vessels in the country at that time. In 1935 there was a fire in one of the sail stores which destroyed all the models and plans of his vessels, so there are no real records of how he designed them. He was also active on the town council and was secretary of the Shipwrecked Fishermen and Mariners' Society. When the oyster beds were contaminated in 1902, he lost more than the other traders, and he sued the council. From his papers it appears that there were £3 million worth of oysters being traded in Emsworth each year, and in one month the trade collapsed. The case went on for some years, and he was tenacious in his pursuit of the council. His other passion – apart from work – was cycling. He was an enthusiastic member of the Emsworth Cycling Club and cycled every day no matter what the weather.

Left: Birky Miller was an original character in Emsworth at the beginning of the twentieth century, who survived by doing odd jobs for anyone. He was well known to everyone because he trained a heron and a duck to follow him around, and he would sit in the Square with them sitting at his feet. When the coaches and carriages came through Emsworth on their way to the races at Goodwood he would entertain the passengers with a song and dance. Here he is riding his assisted bicycle, designed by himself, which allowed him to travel faster than if he just had his pedals.

Below: Don Willshire was landlord of the Bluebell Inn in the 1950s, before it was demolished and reconstructed in its present form. Here he is, the only one with a tie, sitting with Muriel and many of his regular customers. Most of them had worked on the water at one time or another.

Children's parties are always events to be anticipated. Here a group of mums from the Emsworth Young Wives' Club in the 1960s appear to be enjoying it as much as their children.

Amos Boutell came from a line of fishermen who worked on the oyster smacks. His family came from Brightlingsea in Essex, as many of the oystermen did, and his sons continued in his footsteps. He worked for J.D. Foster and skippered some of his larger oyster smacks, including *Echo*.

The gentleman standing in the boat is William Prior, known as Captain Prior. He came from a long line of Emsworth fishermen and was the secretary of the Emsworth Dredgermen's Association: they were the oyster fishermen of Emsworth who tried many times to revive the oyster fishing industry after its slump in 1902. For many years he was retained by Dr French, physician to George V, to skipper his yacht around the world.

In 1961 the ladies of the Mothers' Union were involved in many aspects of the life of Emsworth. Here some of their leading members pose outside Mrs Richardson's house in Warblington Road.

In the 1950s and 1960s the Emsworth retailers and businesses worked together to promote the town. Here some of them are at the presentation to the winners of the annual window-dressing competition.

This line of ladies consists of the Girl Guide Captains and Brown Owls who looked after and instructed the Guides and Brownies of Emsworth in the 1970s and 1980s. Whether they are on parade or waiting to start the race is not sure.

Above: One of the biggest events in the calendar is the Emsworth Food Festival. It is run by a volunteer committee, who plough all the proceeds back into community good causes. Here they are relaxing after the 2005 event, with other helpers. The expressions are a mixture of relief, tiredness and exhaustion.

Left: Eric Lovell was based in the area during the Second World War, and met Joy Whillier. After the war they married and set up in business as 'Fruits', selling fruit and vegetables and providing cut flowers and arrangements. From 1946 until 2005, he was a familiar face in North Street, and was always the first shopkeeper to open in the morning. Here he is dressed as John Bull for the royal wedding in 1981.

Right: The side of all events that the public do not see, the volunteers who give of their time and expertise to make the occasion run smoothly. Here the Emsworth Horticultural Show helpers decide who gets a table.

Below: John Hollis (on the left), who left the Navy and set up Emsworth Rope Shop in the Square: everything from macramé to mooring ropes – if it had knots in it, he would know how to do it. His enthusiasm and support for the Horticultural Society was immense and he was a patient teacher for those learning to ring the bells in Westbourne church.

The man with the microphone is Jim Booth. For many years he was a leading light in the Emsworth Horticultural Society, and led from the front. He lived in Victoria Road and his family still lives in Emsworth. He was known to a whole generation of children as their special lollypop man, who helped them across the road safely.

Dickie Bates took over the Little Green pub and converted it into his 'swap shop'. Here his children pose during one of those long endless days of childhood that we always remember.

No book about Emsworth would be complete without swans. They have been part of every Emsworth child's life for generations. Both mill ponds have their colony of swans and they all love being fed with bread and cakes. Those on the Slipper Pond have bred in the same spot for many years, despite their nesting site being reduced when the short bypass cut through their island. This means that every year they have a smaller area to nest on, and it is now within reach of the foxes who wade out to the island, and the vandals who think it fun to throw stones at them. The swans on the other mill pond leave to breed in the harbour and bring their offspring back later in the year. At any one time there can be between forty and fifty swans around Emsworth. They are used to the ponds being used for other activities, and when the children are practicing their canoe skills in the quiet waters of the ponds they just glide serenely to the other end. They know their adoring fans will find them and feed wherever they are on the water.

Other local titles published by Tempus

Fareham
ALICE JAMES

Since its early days as a quiet country market town, Fareham has continually grown and altered: this fascinating collection of more than 200 old photographs vividly records the Fareham of both the distant past and more recent years. Including images of Price's school, the 'moveable' fire station and the ever-changing streets, shops and churches of the town, *Fareham* will delight all those who know and love the area.

1 8458 8146 X

Haunted Winchester
MATTHEW FELDWICK

Drawing on historical and contemporary sources, *Haunted Winchester* contains a chilling range of ghostly accounts. This selection includes tales of spectral monks at Winchester Cathedral and phantom horses in the Cathedral Close, as well as stories of the Eclipse Inn where Dame Alice Lisle, condemned by Judge Jeffreys, still walks. This phenomenal gathering of ghostly goings-on is bound to captivate anyone interested in the supernatural history of the area.

0 7524 3846 8

Southampton: the Second Selection
A.G.K. LEONARD

This compilation of over 220 photographs documents the many aspects of the social history and development of Southampton from Victorian times to the Second World War. It recalls bygone townscapes, transport and shipping scenes, past occupations, occasions and recreations, and some of the people who have made their distinctive contributions to the growth of the town and port.

07524 2484 X

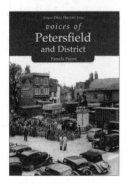

Voices of Petersfield and District
PAMELA PAYNE

This fascinating book brings together the memories of people who have lived and worked in the market town of Petersfield and its surrounding villages during the last century. From the recollections of those who lived 'below stairs' to Dickensian factories, the war years and the day that bulls escaped from Petersfield Market, this intriguing volume, containing over 110 photographs drawn from various private collections, will delight all who know the area.

0 7524 3127 7

If you are interested in purchasing other books published by Tempus, or in case you have difficulty finding any Tempus books in your local bookshop, you can also place orders directly through our website

www.tempus-publishing.com